to the end
of the age."

Matthew 28:20b

GOD IS WITH ME

Always
and Everywhere

Written by Cornelia Mary Bilinsky

Illustrated by Candace Camling

Pauline
BOOKS & MEDIA
Boston

Library of Congress Cataloging-in-Publication Data

Bilinsky, Cornelia Mary.
  God is with me always and everywhere / written by Cornelia Mary Bilinsky ; illustrated by Candace Camling.
    pages cm
  ISBN 978-0-8198-3122-4 -- ISBN 0-8198-3122-0
  1. God (Christianity)--Omnipresence--Juvenile literature. I. Camling, Candace. illustrator. II. Title.
  BT132.B55 2014
  231.7--dc23

                              2013026296

The Scripture quotations contained herein are from the *New Revised Standard Version Bible: Catholic Edition,* copyright © 1989, 1993, Division of Christian Education of the National Council of the Churches of Christ in the United States of America. Used by permission. All rights reserved.

Cover design by Mary Joseph Peterson, FSP

Illustrated by Candace Camling

Published by Pauline Books & Media, 50 Saint Pauls Avenue, Boston, MA 02130-3491

Printed in Korea

GIWM SIPSKOGUNKYO11-30045 3122-0

www.pauline.org

Pauline Books & Media is the publishing house of the Daughters of St. Paul, an international congregation of women religious serving the Church with the communications media.

2 3 4 5 6 7 8 9   19 18 17 16 15

FOR GROWN-UPS

When children are baptized, they are given a candle accompanied by a prayer that they may always keep alive the flame of faith. *God Is with Me: Always and Everywhere* is intended to introduce children to one of the most important foundations of our faith—the awareness of God's presence in every moment and circumstance of our daily lives.

Appealing to children's delight in creation, *God Is with Me* explains that the wonders of our world are signs of the presence of God. Relatable examples teach children that God is present in the love they experience from family and friends. Memorable verses assure children that they have a guardian angel, a heavenly Mother, and Jesus himself at their side, even in difficult times.

Finally, *God Is with Me* presents the Church as a special place to experience the presence of God, and invites children to take the first steps toward recognizing the Church as a wellspring of God's graces.

A child who is attuned to God's presence is more able to develop a vibrant and personal relationship with God. Knowing that God is with me is an essential foundation for the life of faith and good deeds to which we are all called at Baptism.

Parents are entrusted with the awesome responsibility of fostering their children's spiritual growth. *God Is with Me* is meant to help you transmit the immense love of God to the children in your life, and start them on the path to discovering the loving presence of God for themselves.

When I was a little child,
Those who most loved me
Brought me to the church with joy
To join God's family.

I was baptized and I became
A child of God that day;
Now God is with me always,
Everywhere, in every way.

God is with me all around.
The lovely things I see,
Or hear or touch, or taste or smell
Are gifts God made for me.

God is with me in the morning
As I greet the rising sun,
And prepare to spend my day,
Learning, playing, having fun.

God is with me in the daytime
And also through the night,
When the sun has gone to sleep
And twinkling stars give light.

God is with me in my family,
Who give me love and care;
God is with me in the friends
With whom I play and share.

God is with me in the angel
Who stays right by my side
As my special guardian
To watch me and to guide.

9

God is with me in his Mother,
The Virgin Mary fair,
Who from her place in heaven
Helps me with her prayers.

Most of all, my God is with me
In my very best friend—
The Lord Jesus, Son of God,
Who holds me by the hand.

Jesus Christ has been my friend
Since my Baptism day
When he first came to be with me,
And promised he would stay.

He is with me at my church,
Where I join God's family;
As we sing and pray together,
I feel him close to me.

There I hear the word of God
Read from the holy book,
And there are signs of Jesus
Most everywhere I look.

He's in the Holy Eucharist,
The special food he gives,
To make a place within my heart,
Where he wants to live.

Jesus teaches me the way
To be gentle, kind, and good;
To help others, and to share,
And do the things I should.

When I live the JESUS way
With LOVE in all I do,
Then family, friends, and everyone
Can see God's with them too!

But even when I make mistakes
And follow my own will,
Jesus waits with understanding—
And yes, he loves me still.

So God is with me as I grow
And whatever I will be,
God will help me live the life
That he has planned for me.

I am thankful God is with me;
I'll bless and praise his name.
But even if I should forget,
God's with me just the same.

God is with me all my life,
And when my days are done,
I hope to live in heaven
With God, forever on.

FOR KIDS

Dear Children,

May you always know that God is with you.
When you see the wonderful things God has made,
like silver white snowflakes, bright butterflies,
baby robins in their nests,
sandy beaches, and warm summer days,
may your heart be thankful
as you think of God and know that he is very near.
And at those times when you feel so loved,
like when your mom kisses you on your forehead,
or makes you a special birthday cake,
or when your dad plays a game of catch with you,
or when a special friend comes over to play,
or when your grandma sits beside you and tells you
     stories,
may you understand that these are
God's ways of loving you.

When you're frightened, sick, or worried,
may you never forget
that you have a guardian—an angel of God—
and Mary, the Mother of God, who love you.
And may you be sure that you can always pray to
them for help.
But most of all, may you always believe that God is
with you
through his Son, the Lord Jesus Christ,
who became your friend at Baptism.
May you always listen to the teachings of Jesus
and follow his way of love.
When the time comes, may you welcome him in
Holy Communion
and keep him always in your heart,
for it is through Jesus and with Jesus and in Jesus
that you can truly know
that God is with you.

CORNELIA MARY BILINSKY was born and raised in Manitoba. She received her Bachelor of Arts Degree in English and Theology from St. Paul's College at the University of Manitoba. She taught English at the high school level as well as English as a Second Language at a community college. Cornelia's husband is a Ukrainian Catholic priest. They currently reside in Oshawa, Ontario, and have one daughter and one granddaughter. Since 1981, Cornelia has worked alongside her husband at Ukrainian Catholic parishes in Ontario. She most enjoys teaching children about the faith with stories, plays and songs. Cornelia is the author of *Santa's Secret Story* and *The Saint Who Fought the Dragon* (Pauline Kids 2011), *The Queen and the Cross*, (2013), and *God Is with Me* (2014).

CANDACE CAMLING works as a freelance illustrator from her home studio in Des Moines, Iowa. She earned her Bachelor of Fine Arts Degree in Illustration from Kendall College of Art and Design in 2007, and was proud to graduate as valedictorian and winner of the Studio Excellence Award. Candace teaches children's classes at the Des Moines Art Center and enjoys working in watercolor, oils, and digital media. She has done art work for American Greetings, Manley Toy Network, and various other clients as far away as Australia. A member of the Society of Children's Book Writers and Illustrators, Candace's main passion is illustrating for children. *God Is with Me* is her second book with Pauline Kids. Her first was *Santa's Secret Story,* released in 2011.

Who are the Daughters of St. Paul?

We are Catholic sisters. Our mission is to be like Saint Paul and tell everyone about Jesus! There are so many ways for people to communicate with each other. We want to use all of them so everyone will know how much God loves us. We do this by printing books (you're holding one!), making radio shows, singing, helping people at our bookstores, using the Internet, and in many other ways.

Visit our Web site at www.pauline.org

BOOKS & MEDIA

The Daughters of St. Paul operate book and media centers at the following addresses. Visit, call, or write the one nearest you today, or find us at www.pauline.org.

CALIFORNIA
3908 Sepulveda Blvd, Culver City, CA 90230   310-397-8676
935 Brewster Avenue, Redwood City, CA 94063   650-369-4230
5945 Balboa Avenue, San Diego, CA 92111   858-565-9181

FLORIDA
145 S.W. 107th Avenue, Miami, FL 33174   305-559-6715

HAWAII
1143 Bishop Street, Honolulu, HI 96813   808-521-2731

ILLINOIS
172 North Michigan Avenue, Chicago, IL 60601   312-346-4228

LOUISIANA
4403 Veterans Memorial Blvd, Metairie, LA 70006   504-887-7631

MASSACHUSETTS
885 Providence Hwy, Dedham, MA 02026   781-326-5385

MISSOURI
9804 Watson Road, St. Louis, MO 63126   314-965-3512

NEW YORK
64 W. 38th Street, New York, NY 10018   212-754-1110

SOUTH CAROLINA
243 King Street, Charleston, SC 29401   843-577-0175

TEXAS
Currently no book center; for parish exhibits or outreach evangelization, contact: 210-569-0500, or SanAntonio@paulinemedia.com, or P.O. Box 761416, San Antonio, TX 78245

VIRGINIA
1025 King Street, Alexandria, VA 22314   703-549-3806

CANADA
3022 Dufferin Street, Toronto, ON M6B 3T5   416-781-9131

"I will never leave you